**Focus on....**

Managing and getting the most from

Emails

Stephen J. Mordue

Focus on... managing and getting the most from emails.

www.shortsmedia.org

Twitter @sjmordue @swshorts

Facebook @SelfCareshortsSJM
@socialworkshorts

Published by
Shorts Media (Books)
Durham, England

"Finish the job as the sting is often in the tail"
Nassim Nicholas Taleb - Antifragile

ALSO AVAILABLE FROM THE AUTHOR

How to Thrive in Professional Practice
Stephen J. Mordue, Lisa Watson, Steph Hunter
Published by Critical Publishing

How to Thrive at Work
Stephen J. Mordue
(this book is a general audience version of the above book)
Published by Critical Publishing

Social Work: Your Ultimate First Placement (70 day) Reflective Journal
Stephen J. Mordue
Published by Shorts Media (Books)

Social Work: Your Ultimate Final Placement (100 day) Reflective
Journal
Stephen J. Mordue
Published by Shorts Media (Books)

Resilience Workbook: Exploring the Three Pillars of Resilience
Stephen J. Mordue
Published by Shorts Media (Books)

Also

Self Care Shorts YouTube Channel
@selfcareshorts

Social Work Shorts YouTube Channel   @socialworkshorts

For everyone who sent me an email I never responded to.

Send me another. I'll do so much better this time.

Emails!

"I'll just leave that email until later. It'll be fine". We've all said it... you know you have. And sometimes it is fine. And sometimes it isn't, and you think if only I'd taken a couple of minutes to do that then the thing that's just happened wouldn't have happened. I would have headed the problem off. But we procrastinate. I mean, why do today what you can put off until tomorrow!

My favourite procrastination meme says, *"Procrastination is the art of running your life for no apparent reason"*. Yet still we do it. We put it off and it bites us on the backside later. Emails they have an uncanny knack of disappearing from view off the bottom of the screen as our inbox fills up never to be seen again until someone says, "but I emailed you about it". And sure enough they did... and there it is!

The esteemed British economist John Maynard Keynes writing in the 1920's and 30's was convinced that society could sustain itself because of the advances we would see in technology by people working for around 15 hours a week. He said that the problem we would face in the future, the times we are living in now, would be what to do with all our leisure time. What went wrong there!! Most of us seem to have less time than ever and have a constant battle to keep on top of all manner of things including our overflowing email inboxes. It hurts all the more to discover Charles Dickens wrote 15 novels, 200 short stories, edited a weekly magazine and was able to do this without doing any work in the afternoons. (These days, of course, one take on that story would be that if only Dickens had turned up for an afternoon of work, he could have written 30 books and managed two magazines a week).

The writer Cal Newport (Deep Work & A World Without Email) is convinced that we could do our jobs significantly quicker if we changed one simple thing about the way we work. Emails! He says firms hire workers and then give them a connection to attention demanding information networks making it very easy for workers to find themselves spending all day answering emails and doing video calls. At the end of the week, it doesn't feel like much has got done, but we've exhausted ourselves doing it. Newport believes we should just stop using email – *and if we can't.... use it carefully.*

Here's the thing – email is not your job - your job title isn't email manager – email should support your job not feel like it's become your job. And here's one of the 'head shaking', 'goodness yes' problems with email... the way we use email means that getting through your email generates... more email! Here's an interesting piece of information – in open plan offices, designed to stimulate dialogue and collaboration, email traffic goes up! Something is seriously wrong.

Non distracted periods of time are crucial to all jobs – particularly 'knowledge' jobs.

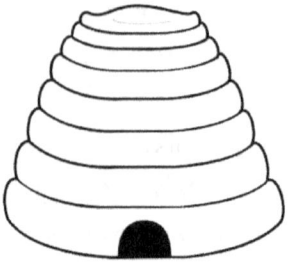

Cal Newport suggests the way the modern world is leads to us having a 'Hive Mind'. A state of mind where our workflow is centred around ongoing conversations fuelled by unstructured and unscheduled messages delivered through digital communication tools like email and messenger services. Busy, busy, busy, like a busy bee always buzzing!

We are always alert to the 'danger' of the next email – always looking for the next thing to emerge out of the undergrowth. This stimulates our stress response – leads to repeated checking and rechecking - and creates a state called hyper-vigilance.

So, our day is centred around this and not our actual job! And let's be honest in most of our jobs how often could something not wait a couple of hours so we can switch email off and get on with some work?

Australian telecoms business research in 2011 found that workers divided their day into an average of 88 'episodes' – 60 dedicated to communication. I'd argue the real work – the work that actually got something done – was somewhere in the other 28 episodes. Task switching depletes psychological capacity leading to a productivity dip due to a cognitive reset every time you shift task. 88 tasks in a 7.5 hour day is 5 minutes a task - what meaningful work can you get done in 5 minutes?

Microsoft research

Email is such an important function in the modern workplace that we need to be able to effectively manage it. Most of us, I believe, work through our emails in a haphazard way 'doing' emails in between other tasks when we get a few minutes. This leads to an inconsistent approach and a feeling of uncertainty about where we are up to. I feel that it is much more productive to set specific timeslots aside to 'do' emails and then when we are not doing them close them down, switch off alerts. To not do these two things mean we are constantly interrupted by incoming emails and we're never sure where we are up to with them.

Control it or it will control you.
David Allen – Getting Things Done. The Art of Stress Free Productivity.

Research undertaken for Microsoft by Iqbal and Horvitz in 2007 gives an interesting insight into how disruption to Deep Work by reading emails can impact on productivity. They asked their programmers to go about their business programming and said they were going to interrupt them with an email. They were then to go and read the email and then return to their programming. They found that after the interruption it took them 10 to 15 minutes to return to focused activity on the task that was originally being undertaken.

They then decided to try another idea. They sent people an email but asked them not to look at it. They found the same attentional problem simply from knowing there was an email there that they found when people actually read the email.

Turn the alerts off!
Do email then shut email down!

*

When the first emails were sent in the early 1970's they were the ultimate easy to use asynchronous tool. I don't need to know where you are but I can send you an email and ask you what I want to know and at some point you'll tell me the answer. I send it when it is convenient to me, and you reply when it is convenient to you. Excellent!

Fast forward to the 2020's and this has morphed to an always on, always alert, notification nightmare. This was never the intention. And now we don't even need to be at our desks because we have our emails on our phones! There's a stupid idea if ever there was one! It's not sustainable.

And now we have the eye icon and the dots in Teams. I know you've seen my message…. so why aren't you replying? I sit and wait. Ah! Here we go the dots start to ripple. I await the response. And all the time I am doing this I am doing… precisely nothing.

We send an email and wait for a response. We don't think they'll get back to me when they can – we want an immediate response. So, we keep checking and rechecking. Hyper vigilance. Stress.

The person at the other end knows this (because they do it as well!) so feel the pressure to respond even though they may well be in the middle of Deep Work. So, they interrupt themselves to respond to your demand and reduce their productivity – leaving them with a problem caused by your problem! And then you email back...... and then they email back... this process of exchange has another name – it's called a conversation. A conversation it's much easier and more efficient if undertaken using the spoken word rather than email.

There are various estimates, but it appears the average person at work sends and receives about 130 emails per day. Daniel Levitin (The Organized Mind) tells us that even outside of work we process around 100,000 words every day.

Gloria Mark (University of California researcher into digital media and its impact) says in some large organisations people check their email 77 times per day – that's an email check less than every six minutes

At best Mark found people went 20 minutes without checking.

Things to bear in mind before we get started.

There are a few things to bear in mind before we get to dealing with our overflowing Inbox and thinking about how to manage and write emails more effectively.

Think carefully before sending an email – because we often don't. In that statement, I feel, lies the nub of the problem. Is email always the best option? Is an email *now* the best option? We have got so used to firing off emails without a second thought it's our default position. And that's not to say it might not be the best option but, as with all things, automatic actions rather than thought through actions are fraught with possible pitfalls. Is email the best way to deal with this conversation? Remember when we used to use the phone!?

That email may arrive on someone's electronic 'desk' at an inopportune moment particularly if they haven't figured out how to switch notifications off – it can be a distraction that we can't resist looking at. And if the person does have alerts off, they may not respond. So, send your email and be patient – stop repeated checking to see if they've responded. They're probably busy.

The dreaded CC function.

"Let's just see how many people we can annoy with this email". "Let's see what cumulative pressure we can place on the person to respond immediately by cc'ing in the big guns – then they can wait with me and see how long it takes!" I suspect we've all done this at some point in our career. It is sometimes necessary but sometimes it's not. Sometimes it can be hostile.

There may be times when it is helpful to copy people in, but we need to think carefully as that is then another email in someone's Inbox that may be of limited use to them and they are left thinking do I need to reply to this or not or is it just for information. Use CC cautiously and never use it to add pressure into the 'system'.

In the same vein think about your use of 'reply all'. Does everyone really need to see what I think about this? Do I even need to reply if I have nothing to say?

Email outside of 'usual' work hours.

Now I'm all for flexible working and people working when it is best for them as far as the job can allow – but it's worth noting that the pressure of receiving an email outside of normal working hours even when the email signature says it's ok not to respond is problematic. Firstly, I suppose, your alerts should be off anyway when you are not working. But work is so ubiquitous these days that emails end up on phones (stop doing this!) and people may well work on other things outside of hours (sometimes their choice and that's fine if it is) and see emails inadvertently or... they can't resist a quick look!

In France originations with more than 50 employees have to have specific policies about email outside of work. This is how it should be. It should be clear what is expected of you and, when, if at all, you should be aware of emails.

In many European countries employees have a legal right to disconnect from the use of digital tools to ensure observance of rest time and leave as well as of personal and family life.

Back to Gloria Marks research...
The longer you spend on email in any given hour the higher your stress levels.

Marks used thermal imaging and heart rate monitors to look for tell-tale signs of stress while people were working and discovered this correlation. Also stressed people respond to emails faster but not better. Linguistic analysis shows that emails sent when anxious have more words that could be construed as 'angry' to the recipient.

Instead of reducing work emails have created more work.

The more emails you reply to…. The more you get back. So, while we are going to explore getting on top of emails, we need to start by thinking about how many we send in the first place and whether this is the best method to employ. We can manage our emails effectively, but it does take time when we could be doing other things. Imagine a conversation conducted by email about a complex decision. How long does it take to write, read, and respond to those emails? Over what time frame are those emails exchanged? Hours? Days? Would a conversation not be more efficient?

When I started in social work there was no email. There was one computer in the corner of each office that got switched on occasionally – and yet the work got done. Then we started using computers more and suddenly some of the job did feel easier, like writing letters and printing them yourself for example, although we still had a typing pool. But then this became a monster, **and** it was an opportunity to get rid of the typing pool! And then this thing that was useful became a thing that you had to do because there was no other way. The work that was being done by two people was now being done by one person. And lo-and-behold further down the line that one person ended up stressed. I wonder why?

Think!

Is email the best way for this message?
Do I really need to cc all of these people in?
Do I really need to 'reply all'?

Find out how to silence alerts!

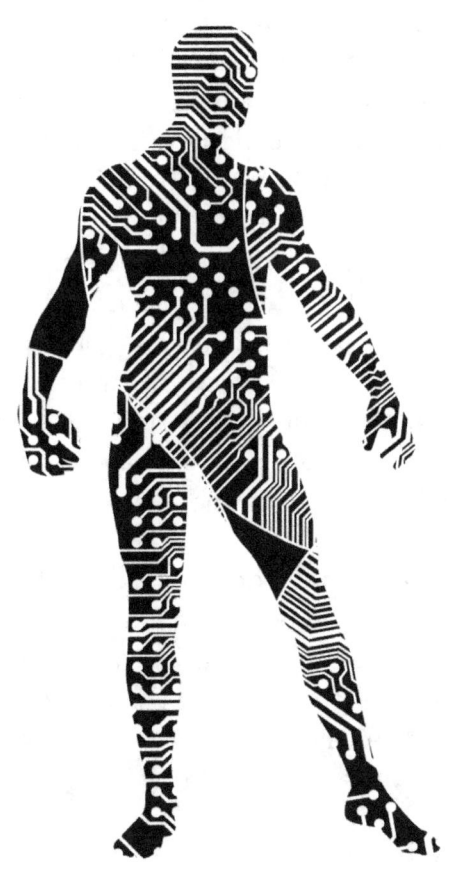

Making a start

David Allen (my favourite productivity guru!) says that your Inbox is a capture tool not a storage solution. Your job on a daily basis should be to 'get in to empty'.

How many emails are in your Inbox at work? Someone told me they had 8000! Each one of those is draining psychologically capacity because each one is something you don't know about (or can't have remembered about) – something that needs to be done and maybe even things that have been done but not filed away ....and you don't know that if the email is still in the numbers in your inbox. I bet for some of you it's hundreds and once they disappear off the bottom of the screen they disappear out of your mind. 'I emailed you about it', 'Don't think I've seen it', 'It was a week or so ago', scroll scroll scroll.... 'Oh, there it is'.

If your Inbox is empty, or at least down to a handful of emails, there can be nothing in there that's more than a few hours old, or a day at most. Imagine opening your inbox every day knowing that there are only new emails in there – the rest is managed somewhere else – not done necessarily – but managed.

We need to start by dealing with the backlog.

Here's why:

Managed – unfinished tasks drain our psychological capacity less than **unmanaged – unfinished tasks** – *if we have controlled the task and put it into a system that will prompt us at a specific time we can forget about the task until prompted. If it's left as an email in our inbox it's an unknown.*

If your Inbox is overflowing set yourself some time aside and systematically work through it. You'll feel great! And then once you are down to a manageable amount, you'll find it easy to keep on top of them. **So, here's what to do!**

Firstly, I am confident, especially in this modern workplace we exist in, that if an email is older than about 3 months your response to it is probably useless or worse embarrassing that it took you a quarter of a year to respond. Now – I think you can probably delete them but.... just in case ...I'm not going to ask you to!

Create a folder in your email programme (see appendix for how to do this). In Outlook it's in New Item/Folder. Call it something like 'Older than 3 months'. Drag anything older than 3 months into this folder and breathe. You can go back to it and work though it if you need or want to. But I'm confident there's probably nothing in there worth worrying about. John in Accounts Payable wouldn't have waited 3 months for a response! (If moving everything older than 3 months is freaking you out you could go for a different numbers of months). This is how I started when I wanted to Reset my emails and... I never went back into that folder... ever.

Now find a space in your calendar when you can dedicate a good period of time to the task of working through the rest. I'd suggest giving yourself a day or half day. If you don't want to do that or you really can't find a half day or a full day, then you are going to have to diary out an hour periodically to work away at it. This is not as effective in my view but if it's what you have to do then it's what you have to do. It will take you longer in the long run because there is a 'start-up' time to get up to speed and remember where you were up to every time.

Before you start create some folders in Outlook. (There are some instructions in the Appendices for creating folders in Outlook). Create a unique folder for all of the projects you are involved in and all of the groups you attend. Try not to go too mad – you don't want hundreds but enough to be able to store emails under a sensible heading.

Also, while we're doing this, I find another few folders useful. I have a folder called Needs Action. In fact, it's actually called *Needs Action* for two reasons. It makes it stand out and, because (if the folder is in your Inbox) it is sorted alphabetically so folders named with symbols at the start appear at the top. (It works the same in normal folders – so things you want to find quickly can appear at the top!) I also have a folder called *Need to Read*.

I then have Monday to Friday folders for emails I need to use on those days - some people utilise a Pending folder.

I then have a folder called Mailing Lists and I have filters set up (see appendices for folder set up) to direct any mailing list emails to this folder.

Ok!! You're good to go and make a start! Work through those emails systematically and get them sorted! Follow the PROCESS I'm about to outline. It's the same process you are going to use every day to keep getting 'in' to 'empty'.

The Process

There's a process you can go through to get in to empty the first time and then all of the subsequent times, day in day out – and it comes to us courtesy of the wonderful David Allen again! When working through your emails, take them each in turn and either 'Do it, Delegate it, Defer it, or Delete it'.

You can start with **Delete it if you like**. Prune first to get rid of anything you don't need or you are not interested in. As you go through things if you are going to delete it think, 'how did I get this in the first place?' Is it a mailing list? If it is you might want to unsubscribe or set a filter to filter it out of your inbox into a separate folder (there are instructions for Outlook in the Appendices). You can also Delete as you are going through the next steps but personally I think you can spot some easy Delete's with a first quick pass and this will probably cut down the numbers and make you feel a whole load better.

Let's have a look at each of the steps in turn.

There will be some things in your Inbox where you can just **'Do it'**. Here's your chance to apply the 2-minute rule. If it's going to take you less than two minutes to do just do it. Don't procrastinate, don't leave it till later... just do it. There's a psychological 'problem' called the planning fallacy that leads us to overestimate how long small tasks will take and underestimate how long big tasks will take. There are lots of emails you can do in two minutes because two minutes is a lot longer than you think. Once you realise how long two minutes is you can use this rule to great effect. If it's going to take longer than this then maybe you need to Defer It.

And when you have dealt with the email either save it off to a project folder for reference or delete it. You're done with it.

The 'Do it' – 2-minute rule strategy reminds me of the OHIO principle…. Only Handle It Once! Sound advice.

The next one is **'Delegate it'**. Delegation is not a 'down the command chain' activity. It is merely passing something on to someone because they need to do something so you can do something, or you need information from them so you can undertake the task. Delegation here means that you need something from someone in order to complete whatever you are being asked to do. You email them and then you are done with that email for now. You have delegated the next action in the process to them. How much you want to keep an eye on the other person and the response you need defines what you do next. If it's of low importance you can move the email into one of your folders. You'll be reminded to do the next thing when the person gets back to you. If you need to keep an eye and make sure that you do get a response you could move it into *Needs Action*. Part of your email strategy needs to be to check the emails in your *Needs Action* folder periodically. If it's hugely important you could put an entry in your calendar on the day you want to chase the email up to tell you to do that – and put it in one of your days of week folder. Control it or it will control you!

Sometimes you may need to do some work in order to respond to an email or, the email may have given you a task to work on. So, you **'Defer It'** into what Allen calls a Trusted System. Your Trusted System is likely to be your calendar – mine is. But depending on your role it may be other things. Essentially your Trusted System is the system that keeps track of everything in your workload (or in your life as well if you are so inclined... I am!) Everything needs to be in there. For you to be able to trust a trusted system it needs to be complete. It needs to include everything that you are responsible for, everything you need to do, or you will find it very hard to trust it. Knowing what you need to do next is largely about knowing what you can safely not do next. That's David Allen again!

For me, if things are time and date specific, they go in my calendar in a time and date slot. If something is actionable but not time and date specific it goes into my calendar as an 'all day' event on a day where

I might be able to get to it. See appendix for how to do this.

If something needs some thought and planning and isn't time and date specific it goes into my spreadsheet (you could use a word document, notebook, or anything really – as long as it helps you keep track). Once it's in one of those places I save or delete the email. Remember to go back to your spreadsheet or other tool periodically. You guessed it – put a check point in your calendar as a recurring event.

Also utilise that *Need to Read* folder for stuff that's interesting… papers, web sites, videos (I know you don't read them, but you see what I mean!). Pop something in your dairy once a week that nudges you to go and have a look and actually read something!

Once you've Deferred the Task into your workflow system you need to move the email. You can use your *Needs Action* folder or one of your **daily folders** or you may be able to delete it. If there's not much information in the email that you need you could cut and paste it into the Notes section of the task in your calendar (see appendix for how to do this) and 'file' or delete the email. I leave little helpful notes in the task for myself like *Write Report for Jane – see email in Needs Action –* so I know where to go for what I need. The key is – don't leave it in your Inbox!

Finally, in this process, if something isn't for you or of interest to you **'Delete It'**! Go on you'll feel good! Remember you've got your Need to Read folder if you don't feel comfortable doing the delete – you could have a Might Like to Read folder as well or a Maybe I Should Delete folder!?

Emails! They are necessary but you can manage them. Having them under control will reduce stress and allow you to focus on other tasks without worrying about what's in there!

Now comes the easy part...

How to keep 'In' empty

First rule!

Manage your email time like it's a task – set time to do emails.

Email is an activity that you need to do in a focused way not just something you do when you get a chance. You are going to do emails at two key points in the day. First thing in the morning and last thing at the end of the day. Once you get into the habit of this 'first thing in the morning' gets easier and easier as the only things that have arrived are the things that arrived late in the day after you went home. Depending on your role a midday check can also be useful. I use a midday check but only to see if there's anything urgent.

Set aside however much time you think you need to get in to empty. I set aside half an hour in the morning and half an hour in the afternoon. I sometime need longer so there's slippage around the afternoon one. Remember you are not necessarily doing everything you are managing everything.

When you are *not* actively dealing with emails close your email down and switch off alerts. There is lots of research evidence to suggest that responding to emails when trying to do other tasks slows you down on the other tasks. There is also evidence that even just knowing there's an email there drags your attention away from focused work.

At your allotted time every day you use the 'do it, delegate it, defer it, delete it, approach' and get your Inbox to Empty. If you miss one of these slots because of other things, then doing it when the chance comes around next time in your diary becomes doubly important. My advice is protect this email time with your life *(well… not quite… but you get what I mean)* or your email will escalate out of control very easily. Put this email time in your calendar as a repeating event. DO NOT leave it to chance! Put it in your calendar. See Appendix for creating repeating events in Calendar)

'Writing' things down gives momentum to the task (honestly! – well researched) and the calendar entry will nag at you to do it. Schedule longer on a Friday afternoon just in case things have got a little 'untidy' so that you can get it sorted. I also have a weekly entry in my diary on a Wednesday (that's when it works best for me) that says Check *Needs Action* and *Need to Read* folder.

And then keep going…. *I'm not going to lie – it's a tough task.* We get far too many emails which is why Inboxes get out of control, but the essential thing is 'Control It or It will Control You' (David Allen again!)

Writing Emails

One message per email

Emails with more than one message in them create opportunities for later things to be missed – leading to, 'well…it was in the email', conversations, leading to people feeling they aren't in control or feelings of inadequacy.

Get the 'ask' in first.

Make sure you ask for what you want in the first sentence. Make it clear. Don't waffle for a paragraph or two then ask your question. *I need to meet with you about project x. I need to talk to you about x. Can we meet?*

Use emails for direct closed questions and planning things

Don't use emails for conversations. Emails are great for saying, 'what time is the meeting on Thursday', but not good for, 'here are some things I want to cover in the meeting on Thursday – here's what I think about this thing – what do you think? I'd like to raise this thing do you think that would be helpful'. These conversations should not be taking place by email. It takes you much longer to type a response than say it because when you do that you read and re-read it – or maybe you don't – which is just as dangerous – and in any sort of discussion or negotiation most of what is going on needs to be guided by not only words but body language or at least the intonation in voice. If an email is more than a few lines, then it's a conversation – so have a conversation.

Write emails that contain options to cut down traffic.

'Can we meet – here are all of the dates I'm available over the next week', is much better than, 'can we meet'.

Ask people to use 'reply all' when trying to organise a number of people – remind people of this. For other sorts of emails ask do I need to do reply all. Think carefully before using cc.

Write emails that people want to read.

A few lines long is enough. Use simple language, short sentences, and snappy phrases.

Long emails

Avoid them! If I have to write a long email I have been known to say – 'sorry this is long but please read all the way to the end – apologies!'

If you have to write a long email do the following –

- As above get the 'ask' in in the first sentence.
- Use short paragraphs.
- Bullet point content at the start.
- Use bold and italics to highlight things. Draw people's attention to the key points. This is good for key dates and times.
- If it's time critical say so – and give a time. If it's not time critical – still give a time! This helps everyone to know where they are and what is expected (this can apply to all emails).
- Find better ways to have conversations because that's what a long email is going to initiate.

Things to consider.

As an organisation figure out how to give people space to move into Deep Work and then don't interrupt them. This is a win-win for the person and the organisation – they'll get things done with greater efficiency.

Use the 'delay send' feature (see appendix for how to do this) when working outside of normal hours. So even if you write it on a night or a weekend it doesn't go until 8 on the next working day.

Never respond to emails when tired and/or emotional. Write the email and then save as a 'draft'. You may well find you later delete the email when you re-read it.

Can't respond to an email – email to say you can't.... 'I really want to spend some time replying and will get to it on....'

'Mine' your email for important information and have a place to store this in a logical fashion. Phone numbers, postal addresses, line management structures, relationships, working hours, on-site days – those kind of things.

Use dictation. You can dictate faster than you can type even if you're a good typist and even though you have to go back and check it over it's generally quicker. If you've not used this for a while have another go. It has got a lot more accurate.

Take action immediately!

If you're fired up right now, then make a start – or at least make a plan. The longer you leave it the less chance you will do it – and this book will become a distant memory of a time you thought there might be an actual chance of you changing something!

Go on! Make the change!

Focus on... managing and getting the most from emails.

Useful Books/References

Allen, D. (2015) Getting Things Done: *The Art of Stress-free Productivity* London: Piatkus

Levitin, D. (2015) *The Organized Mind: Thinking Straight in the Age of Information Overload.* St.Ives: Penguin

Newport, C. (2016) *Deep Work* St.Ives: Piatkus

Newport, C. (2021) *A World Without Email* Dublin: Penguin Random House

Iqbal, S.T. & Horvitz, E. (2007) Disruption and Recovery of Computing Tasks: Field Study, Analysis, and Directions *CHI 2007,* April 28–May 3, 2007, San Jose, California, USA.

Focus on... managing and getting the most from emails.

Appendix: Creating Folders in Microsoft Outlook

Organising your email inbox with folders is an effective way to keep your messages sorted and easily accessible. Microsoft Outlook provides a simple process for creating folders to help you categorize and manage your emails. Follow the steps below to create folders in Microsoft Outlook:

1. Launch Microsoft Outlook: Open Microsoft Outlook on your computer. Ensure that you are in the "Mail" view, where you can see your inbox and other folders.

2. Access the Folder List: Locate the navigation pane on the left side of the Outlook window. If you don't see the navigation pane, click on the "View" tab at the top, and make sure "Folder Pane" is selected. The navigation pane displays a list of folders in Outlook.

3. Choose a Location: Determine where you want to create the new folder. You can create folders directly under your mailbox (e.g., your email address) or within an existing folder to create a subfolder.

4. Create a New Folder: Right-click on the location where you want to create the new folder. In the context menu that appears, select "New Folder." Alternatively, you can go to the "Folder"

tab at the top and click on the "New Folder" button in the "New" group.

5.   Name the Folder: A dialog box will open, prompting you to enter a name for the new folder. Type a descriptive name for the folder that reflects its purpose or category (e.g., "Work," "Personal," "Projects," "Travel," etc.).

6.   Choose Folder Type: Under the "Folder contains" section in the dialog box, select the appropriate folder type. For most folders, the default selection of "Mail and Post Items" will be suitable. However, you can choose other options like "Calendar Items" or "Contact Items" if you plan to store specific types of items in the folder.

7.   Specify Folder Location (Optional):   If you want to create a subfolder within an existing folder, select the desired parent folder from the "Select where to place the folder" drop-down list. By default, the new folder will be created at the root level.

8.   Click "OK":   Once you've entered the folder name and made any desired selections, click the "OK" button to create the folder.

9.   Organise and Customize Folders: After creating folders, you can drag and drop emails from your inbox or other folders into the newly created folders. Right-click on folders to access

options such as renaming, deleting, or changing the folder's colour for visual identification.

By creating folders in Microsoft Outlook, you can organise your emails based on specific categories, projects, or priorities, making it easier to locate and manage your messages. This approach enhances productivity and helps maintain a clutter-free inbox.

Please note that the steps provided are based on Microsoft Outlook 2019, and the process may vary slightly depending on your specific version of Outlook. Refer to the Outlook Help documentation or Microsoft support resources for more detailed instructions if needed.

Appendix: Filtering Mailing List Emails into a "Mailing Lists" Folder in Microsoft Outlook

Managing mailing list emails efficiently can be a challenge, but Microsoft Outlook provides a powerful filtering feature to help you organize your inbox. By creating a dedicated folder called "Mailing Lists" and setting up filters, you can automatically redirect mailing list emails to this folder, keeping your inbox clutter-free and allowing easy access to these messages when needed. Follow the steps below to set up this filtering system in Microsoft Outlook:

1. Create a "Mailing Lists" Folder: Open Microsoft Outlook and navigate to the folder list. Right-click on the location where you want to create the new folder (e.g., under "Inbox" or "Personal Folders") and select "New Folder." Name it "Mailing Lists" or any preferred name that clearly indicates its purpose.

2. Identify Mailing List Senders: Review your inbox and identify the email addresses or domains from which you receive mailing list emails. These are typically newsletters, subscriptions, or group mailing lists.

3.   Set Up Email Rules in Microsoft Outlook: Follow these steps to create a rule to filter mailing list emails:

   a.   Open the Rules and Alerts Window: In Microsoft Outlook, click on the "File" tab at the top left corner, then select "Manage Rules & Alerts."

   b.   Create a New Rule: In the "Rules and Alerts" window, click on the "New Rule" button to start creating a new rule.

   c.   Choose a Template or Start from a Blank Rule: In the "Rules Wizard" window, you can choose to apply a template or create a rule from scratch. Select "Apply rule on messages I receive" and click "Next."

   d.   Specify Conditions: In the next window, specify the conditions for filtering mailing list emails. You can choose to filter based on specific email addresses, domains, or keywords found in the subject or body of the email. For example, you might set the condition to filter emails from "[newsletter@example.com](mailto:newsletter@e xample.com)" or emails containing the word "newsletter" in the subject.

   e.   Choose an Action: Select the action to be performed when the rule conditions match. Choose the option to "Move the item to folder" and click on the "Mailing Lists" folder you created in step 1.

f.   Apply Exceptions (Optional):   If there are any exceptions to the rule, such as specific senders or emails you want to exclude from the filtering, specify them in the next window. Otherwise, click "Next."

g.   Specify Rule Name and Options: Provide a name for the rule (e.g., "Mailing List Filter") and choose any additional options you prefer. Click "Finish" to complete the rule setup.

4.   Test and Refine: After setting up the rule, it's important to test it by subscribing to a sample mailing list or newsletter and sending a test email. Verify that the email is correctly filtered into the "Mailing Lists" folder. If not, revisit the rule settings and make any necessary adjustments.

5.   Manage and Review the Folder: Regularly review the contents of the "Mailing Lists" folder to ensure important emails aren't missed. Unsubscribe from any mailing lists that are no longer relevant or useful to maintain an organized inbox.

 By filtering mailing list emails into a dedicated "Mailing Lists" folder in Microsoft Outlook, you can streamline your inbox and focus on important and personal messages while still having easy access to newsletters and subscription content. This approach allows you to maintain control over your email flow and ensures that important messages don't get lost in the clutter.

Please note that the steps provided are based on Microsoft Outlook 2019, and the process may vary slightly depending on your specific version of Outlook. Refer to the Outlook Help documentation or Microsoft support resources for more detailed instructions if needed.

Appendix: Creating Events in Microsoft Outlook

Effectively managing your schedule and appointments is crucial for efficient email management. Microsoft Outlook provides powerful features to help you create and organize events, whether they are time and date-specific or all-day events. Follow the steps below to create events in Microsoft Outlook:

Creating a Time and Date-Specific Event:

1.   Launch Microsoft Outlook: Open Microsoft Outlook on your computer and navigate to the Calendar view.

2.   Select the Date and Time: In the Calendar view, navigate to the desired date and time for your event. Click and drag to select the time range during which the event will take place.

3.   Create the Event: Once you have selected the desired time range, double-click on the selected area. This will open a new event window.

4.   Enter Event Details: In the event window, enter the relevant details such as the event title, location, and any additional information you want to include.

5. Set Start and End Time: Specify the start and end time of the event by selecting the appropriate time in the "Start time" and "End time" fields.

6. Choose a Reminder (Optional):   If you want to set a reminder for the event, click on the "Reminder" drop-down menu and select the desired reminder time.

7. Save the Event: Once you have entered all the necessary details, click the "Save & Close" button to save the event to your calendar.

Creating an All-Day Event:

1. Launch Microsoft Outlook: Open Microsoft Outlook on your computer and navigate to the Calendar view.

2. Select the Date: In the Calendar view, navigate to the desired date for your all-day event.

3. Create the Event: Right-click on the selected date, and in the context menu that appears, choose "New All Day Event." This will open a new event window.

4.   Enter Event Details: In the event window, enter the relevant details such as the event title, location, and any additional information you want to include.

5.   Set the Event as All-Day: In the event window, ensure that the "All Day Event" checkbox is selected. This will automatically set the start and end time to cover the entire day.

6.   Choose a Reminder (Optional):   If you want to set a reminder for the event, click on the "Reminder" drop-down menu and select the desired reminder time.

7.   Save the Event: Once you have entered all the necessary details, click the "Save & Close" button to save the event to your calendar.

By creating time and date-specific events and all-day events in Microsoft Outlook, you can effectively manage your schedule and appointments. These features allow you to stay organized, set reminders, and ensure you don't miss important events or commitments.

Please note that the steps provided are based on Microsoft Outlook 2019, and the process may vary slightly depending on your specific version of Outlook. Refer to the Outlook Help documentation or Microsoft support resources for more detailed instructions if needed.

Appendix: How to add a note to a calendar entry in Microsoft Outlook:

1. Open Microsoft Outlook on your computer.

2. Navigate to the calendar view by clicking on the "Calendar" button or selecting the calendar icon from the navigation pane.

3. Locate the calendar entry to which you want to add a note. You can find it by browsing through the calendar or using the search function.

4. Double-click on the calendar entry to open it in a new window.

5. In the calendar entry window, you will find a text field labelled "Add a note" or "Notes." Click on this field to activate it.

6. Type in your desired note or additional information for the calendar entry. You can include relevant details, reminders, or any other information that will help you remember important aspects of the event.

7. After adding the note, you can format the text using the options available in the formatting toolbar, such as font styles, size, colour, and alignment.

8. If you want to add multiple paragraphs or line breaks within your note, use the Enter/Return key to create new lines.

9. Once you have entered the note, click on the "Save" button or simply close the calendar entry window to save the changes.

Your note will now be associated with the specific calendar entry in Outlook. You can refer back to it whenever you need to view or edit the note by following the same steps to open the calendar entry and accessing the note field.

Remember to customize these instructions to match the specific version of Microsoft Outlook you are using, as the user interface and features may vary slightly across different versions.

Appendix: How to add a repeating event to a calendar entry in Microsoft Outlook:

1. Open Microsoft Outlook on your computer.

2. Navigate to the calendar view by clicking on the "Calendar" button or selecting the calendar icon from the navigation pane.

3. Locate the date and time for the initial occurrence of the event in the calendar.

4. Double-click on the desired date and time to create a new calendar entry. This will open the appointment window.

5. In the appointment window, enter the details of the event such as the subject, location, and any other relevant information.

6. Next, locate the "Repeat" button or option, which is usually found in the toolbar at the top of the window. Click on it to open the "Appointment Recurrence" or "Recurring Appointment" dialog box.

7. In the "Appointment Recurrence" dialog box, you will find various options to configure the recurring pattern for the event. Choose the options that suit your needs. Here are some common options:

- "Start" and "End" dates: Specify the date range for the repeating event. By default, it will be set to the current date.

- "Pattern" section: Select the frequency of the event occurrence, such as daily, weekly, monthly, or yearly. Choose the appropriate options and set the interval between each occurrence.

- "Range of recurrence" section: Choose whether the event should continue indefinitely or have a specific end date.

8. As you adjust the settings, you can preview the recurring pattern in the "Preview" section of the dialog box.

9. Once you have configured the repeating pattern, click the "OK" or "Save" button to apply the changes and close the dialog box.

10. Back in the appointment window, you can add any additional details or notes related to the specific occurrence of the event, if needed.

11. Finally, click the "Save" button to save the recurring event to your calendar.

Your repeating event will now be added to the calendar in Microsoft Outlook, and it will appear based on the recurring pattern you specified. You can view and manage the series of events by clicking on any occurrence in the calendar or by opening the appointment window.

Please note that the steps provided are general guidelines and may vary slightly depending on the version of Microsoft Outlook you are using. It's recommended to refer to the specific instructions for your Outlook version or consult the Outlook Help documentation for more detailed information.

Appendix: How to use the Delay Send feature in Microsoft Outlook:

1. Open Microsoft Outlook on your computer.

2. Compose a new email by clicking on the "New Email" button or selecting the appropriate option from the toolbar.

3. Enter the email's recipients, subject, and compose the content of your message as you normally would.

4. Before sending the email, locate the "Options" tab in the email composition window. The "Options" tab is typically available at the top of the window.

5. Within the "Options" tab, you will find a button or section labelled "Delay Delivery" or "Delay Send." Click on this button or access this section to open the "Properties" or "Message Options" dialog box.

6. In the "Properties" or "Message Options" dialog box, you will find an option to "Do not deliver before." Check the box next to this option.

7. Specify the date and time when you want the email to be sent. You can either type the desired date and time or use the date picker and time selection controls provided.

8. Once you have set the desired delivery time, click the "Close" or "OK" button to save the changes and close the dialog box.

9. Complete the remaining steps to address the email and attach any necessary files or documents.

10. When you are ready to send the delayed email, click the "Send" button as you normally would.

11. Outlook will hold the email in the Outbox folder until the specified delivery time arrives. At that time, the email will be sent automatically.

The Delay Send feature in Microsoft Outlook allows you to compose emails in advance and schedule them to be sent at a later time. This feature is particularly useful for managing time-sensitive messages, coordinating different time zones, or ensuring that your emails are sent at an appropriate time.

Please note that the steps provided are general guidelines and may vary slightly depending on the version of Microsoft Outlook you are using. It's recommended to refer to the specific instructions for your Outlook version or consult the Outlook Help documentation for more detailed information.

Appendix: How to use dictation in Microsoft Outlook:

1. Open Microsoft Outlook on your computer.

2. Create a new email, reply to an existing email, or open a draft that you wish to dictate.

3. Place the cursor in the body of the email where you want the dictated text to appear.

4. Locate the "Dictate" button or option in the Outlook toolbar. In newer versions of Outlook, this button may have a microphone icon. Click on it to activate the dictation feature.

5. If prompted, grant permission for Outlook to access your microphone.

6. Begin speaking clearly and naturally. Outlook will convert your speech into text in real-time and insert it into the email.

7. As you dictate, you can include punctuation marks and formatting commands by speaking them aloud. For example, you can say "comma," "full-stop," "new paragraph," or "bold" to include those elements in the text.

8. If you need to correct any errors or make changes, you can use the keyboard or the mouse to navigate and edit the text.

9. To pause the dictation, click the "Dictate" button again or use the designated pause command, such as saying "pause" or "stop dictation."

10. If you want to resume dictation after pausing, click the "Dictate" button again and continue speaking.

11. Once you have finished dictating the email, review and edit the text as necessary.

12. Complete the remaining steps, such as adding recipients, subject, and any additional attachments or formatting.

13. When you are ready to send the email, click the "Send" button as you normally would.

Using dictation in Outlook can help improve productivity and efficiency by allowing you to quickly compose emails using your voice. It's especially useful for individuals who prefer speaking over typing or need to dictate longer emails.

Please note that the availability and functionality of the dictation feature may depend on the version of Microsoft Outlook you are using. Additionally, ensure that your computer has a working microphone and that you have granted the necessary permissions for Outlook to access it.

Remember to customize these instructions to match the specific version of Microsoft Outlook you are using, as the user interface and features may vary slightly across different versions.

Focus on... managing and getting the most from emails.

EXTRAS

Applying the 2-minute rule in practice – a beginner's guide!

(Originally published as a blog in March 2021)

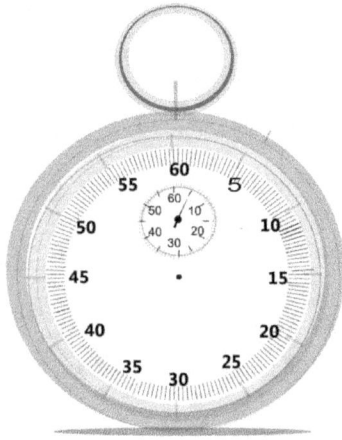

Every time I ask people to feed back to me after the sessions I do about self-care and productivity about what they found most helpful they always mention the 2-minute rule. So... I always talk about it.

It's basically this. If you look at a task and you think it's going to take less than two minutes to complete, then simply do it. Don't delay, don't put it off until later, just do it. You can actually achieve a lot more in two minutes than you think you can. If you have the time, sit quietly now for two minutes. It feels like forever! You could get a lot of small tasks done in that time!

At a session recently though someone suggested that the application of the two minute rule was in contradiction to my view that when immersed in Deep Work we should do it to the exclusion of all other tasks. *"Surely the two-minute rule contradicts this as if you come across something to do then you are suggesting I just do it"*, the person said (I'm paraphrasing – but that was the gist of it I think). I answered something to the effect that the two-minute rule was effective for emails and planning tasks and working through small tasks but not when engaged in deep work. I wasn't satisfied with my explanation. I didn't feel it was clear enough, so I thought I'd write a blog.

There are times, like anything, when the application of an idea is helpful and times when it is unhelpful. The two-minute rule falls into that category. I thought the best way to explain when to use it and when not to use it would be to take you through a typical day of mine and explore the application of this 'rule'.

We all have a start-up strategy. Yes? This is the process that gets you going when you get to work. Just like a computer you need to be powered on and have your software loaded and get yourself ready for the day. My start-up strategy goes like this.

8.30 Open notebook to new page and write the date at the top then Open calendar. Work through the day visualising myself undertaking each task. In doing so I am connecting with the task and checking that I have everything to hand that I need for each task. This is a perfect opportunity to *apply the two-minute rule.* If I find I haven't got something I need for a task, maybe I haven't created a Teams Meeting link or printed off some lecture notes or found a phone number I need, I apply the two-minute rule and do it there and then. Anything else that's longer than two minutes gets put in a time slot in my calendar (this doesn't happen very often, if at all, as my planning strategy means that the big things required are all done)

9.00 Open Emails and work on getting my Inbox to empty. I work through my emails methodically one by one using the Do It, Delegate It, Defer It, Delete It process. The Do It part relies exclusively on *the two-minute rule.* Can I deal with this email in less than two minutes? If I can it gets done there and then. If it's going to take longer than two minutes, it gets deferred into my trusted system.

Working day

9.30 Clearing up and small jobs. This is a good slot for anything that might have fallen out of my diary scan and my emails. If something needed doing urgently, I will have put it into this time slot. No two-minute rule things here I'd imagine because this will be a longer task or tasks that needs doing.

10.00 Deliver lecture. Off I go to do what I do. This is in many ways Deep Work. I'll explain. Deep Work in the productivity literature is usually a job that needs you to be completely focussed to the exclusion of everything else and is usually best undertaken in glorious isolation – distraction free. Now that doesn't define lecturing as you do it in front of people, but I feel it is still a Deep Work task as it requires me to be completely in the moment to the exclusion of everything else. So, no two-minute rule activities going on here.

12.00 At the end of the lecture a student asks me for a tutorial. Yes indeed! Let's plan that now. I have my calendar on my phone. *Two-minute rule* applied tutorial booked. I could have said I'll get back to you later with some times, but no, there and then – let's get this sorted – done and forgotten about – my calendar will remind me of what I need to know.

13.00 Lecture Preparation (after lunch of course as a lunch break is so important). This is Deep Work. I need to be in a quiet place, and I need to be not distracted. I won't be applying the two-minute rule here because i will have switched my phone and emails to silent and I'll be getting on with the task.

But disaster – there is a problem here. Our minds just don't stay focussed on the thing we are doing no matter how hard we try. The more we do Deep Work and the more we train ourselves towards mindful behaviour the better we get at it but nevertheless sometimes something pops into our heads! This is what I refer to as a boundary moment. A point where we have a choice to make about how to proceed! What do we do! *My brain has just reminded me that I was asked by my manager to email them the contact details of someone.*

Now, that could be achieved using the two-minute rule because it will take me less than two minutes to do that. But there's a problem here because opening my emails and sending the information will only take that time up but I might see other emails that interest me – our minds are terrible like that – and I might end up replying because – well – I could do it in two minutes. We become trapped in our emails and the Deep Work gets interrupted and then, when we go back to the Deep Work, it takes (as an experiment conducted by Microsoft found out) 10 to 15 minutes to get back up to speed on the Deep Work task. *So that's not a good idea!*

I could still decide to go and apply the two-minute rule and get the email sent. It might be something really urgent and therefore the interruption may be necessary. I might have to accept the productivity dip.

But if it's not urgent I should resist the urge to send the email now and continue with the Deep Work.

But problem number two raises itself! Every time I try to get on with the Deep Work task, I keep thinking I mustn't forget to send that email! Argh! David Allen calls these Open Loops. They just go round and round in your head taking up vital psychological capacity and distract you from the task in hand. Here's what to do. Externalise your memory and make a note of what needs to be done in your notebook that sits next to you all the time with today's date at the top of the page. You sorted this out at 8.30 this morning during your Start Up strategy! *Note: Send email to manager with contact details for Dave.* This gets it out of your head into your trusted system so that you will be reminded to do it later. It does create a pause, it does create a shifting of attention, but you have minimised it as best you can. We can't help these thoughts encroaching, but we can decide how to manage them for the best.

15.00 Team Meeting. I class this as a Deep Work task as well. The meeting needs my attention so no two-minute rule opportunities here. The same rules apply that we utilised when we were doing lecture prep Deep Work. As you go through the meeting take notes about things you need to to do so we can move them into our trusted system later.

Shut down strategy.

16.00 Emails. This is the same process that we undertook at 9 a.m. Open up those emails work through them and get that Inbox to empty!

16.30 Planning. Getting into empty is not just about that Inbox it's also about that notebook and all of the entries you've made as the day has gone on. You work your way methodically down the list and use the same Do It, Delegate It, Defer It, Delete It process that you used for emails. *Note: Send email to manager with contact details for Dave. Two-minute rule application!* This is where that deferred task gets done in two minutes having caused the minimum of disruptions to your Deep Work. Then, go through the other tasks that you've noted in the same way. They either get done, get deleted, get delegated to others for more information, or get moved into your trusted system as entries in your calendar. Cross them out as you go – it's soooo satisfying! ***Finally plan tomorrow.*** Have you got everything you need for everything you need to do. Get all of your ducks in a row.

17.00 Reflect on the day. *What didn't go so well.* Could you have controlled something better or could you not have foreseen what went wrong. If you could have done something better jot down what you could have done. This helps consolidate your thinking. If you couldn't have predicted what went wrong, then let it go. It is what it is. *Then think about the things that went well, and the things you got done.* This is especially important if you have had a stressful day (....there are other sorts of days I hear you say!) When we are stressed we tend to take a micro view of our day, homing in on small details and this can lead to negative thinking. Get your wide angled lens on and take a birds eye view of the day and enjoy the things that went well.... and then *Shutdown Complete.*

Like any technique it only works in the right circumstances. The two-minute rule needs to be used when it is appropriate and not used indiscriminately when it will interrupt your Deep Work. Unless of course the thing that popped into your head is so important that you should interrupt what you are doing and get it done!

Making a start is the hardest part...

(Originally published as a blog in September 2019)

I've had a job to do for weeks. A report to write. I need to have it done for a meeting tomorrow. And I've kept putting it off! Why!? Once I got down to it I actually enjoyed writing it and it took me about an hour an a half... that was all... and now it's done and I feel great!

Caroline Webb in her great, highly recommended book, How to Have a Good Day, says that most of the jobs we avoid are ones that have a long-term benefit. This report I had to write had no short-term benefit in doing it a few weeks back but now, given the meeting is tomorrow (!) it does have a short term benefit. This, Webb tells us, is an evolutionary mechanism that sees the trade-off between short term and long-term benefits lead to procrastination. She says, "it's easier for our brains to assess the known present than to consider the unknown future" (pg. 104) so we tend to give more priority to the here and now than to the future.

The problem with this is that it means things get left until the last minute. What if something had happened this morning that meant I couldn't write the report. I'd have either had to stay up late (never the time to do your best work) or look unprofessional tomorrow. I say to my adult children that there are 3 things that get you to where you need to be – the first two you will recognise – inspiration and perspiration. But there's a third – reputation – particularly in professional work where people expect you to 'show up' ready to go. Don't let yourself down by not leaving enough time to get the job done so you are prepared.

Picturing the benefits, Webb goes on to say, is the way to beat procrastination. For me, in this example, the benefit would have been a job done, ticked off my list, and not waking up every day for the last week or so thinking I must do that report. What we know is having 'open loops', as David Allen (The Getting Things Done Methodology) calls them erodes your psychological capital. An open loop is a thing that goes round and round in your brain that gets in the way of focussing on the task in hand. So, by not doing the report I have a constant nagging 'you need to do that report' going around in my head when I should be applying my psychological capacity to other things! This is downside of inaction.

What is useful for some larger tasks is to break them down into smaller tasks. So with regard to the report, I needed to write. I needed to find the document online and appraise what I needed to do. I needed to read some evidence that I needed to be aware of to write the report, and then I needed to write the report. A concept called "The Power of Small Wins" tells me that if I'd broken it down into steps a few things happen. The first step suddenly seems more manageable than the whole task and then when each step is completed you get a psychological buzz of satisfaction. If you leave it as one big task you only get the buzz when the task is finished. Psychological boosts at the end of each step motivate you to move onto the next step.

Easy!

- So, break the task down into small steps and diary them all.
- By putting them all in your diary you remove them from your brain – so they are no longer an 'open loop'. You will get to the step in your dairy and be reminded of what to do – you don't need to remember what to do when.
- Plan a 'pay-off'. If it's something you really are struggling to get on with plan a treat

when it's done, or a little treat when each step gets done. Treats are good!
- Consider the downside of not taking action – this may well motivate you.
- Remember – we often overestimate how long something is going to take. I set aside 3 hours to write the report (it had turned into a monster in my head) and it actually only took an hour and a half! I suddenly had some free time... so I wrote this blog!

Two things done when I thought I'd only get one done!
Now that's productivity!

Think big, start small, begin now...

(Originally published as a blog in September 2019)

Recently I got to wondering when I started setting myself big long-term goals and I realised I've probably always done it. Most productivity commentators will tell you that you should have at least a 5-year plan. Personally, I think you need a life plan! What is it you want to do, next week, next month, next year, the rest of your life!? Planning stuff and writing it down has been shown to make it more likely to happen. If you have a plan written down it sets it in your mind. You can refer back to it and when you're ready break your plan down into manageable steps.

Starting with think big – what is that you want to achieve. I remember my first day at college studying social work, listening to my first lecture, and thinking about her, "I want to do what you're doing." And 13 years later I found myself doing just that thing. When I started being a lecturer, I decided I wanted to write and here I am 7 years later writing regularly about social work and a book in the pipeline! It's important to have a growth mind set. In her book Mindset, Dr. Carol S. Dweck tells us that people fall into two categories – those with a fixed mindset and those with growth mindset. If you have a fixed mindset you think that talent and ability is inherent. It's something you either have or you don't have. You think that you're either intelligent or you not. But what Dweck shows in her book is that we can all do whatever we set our minds to. What it takes is hard work and dedication. Things aren't easy but things are achievable if you have a plan and you apply yourself to that plan. Broadly speaking we all have the same potential, it's our mindset that dictates what we do with that potential. So you need to think big! What do you want to achieve?

Then you break it down into small steps. Because, if you had to eat a whole elephant, the only way to do it would be one bite at a time! Those steps need to be small and achievable. By breaking things down into little steps you draw on the psychological power of small wins. Every time you complete a step you get a psychological buzz! A feel-good boost. If you don't break things down into small tasks, firstly you won't know where to start or what to do next. And secondly, you will only get to feel that buzz when you achieve the final goal. Write down the goal, break it down into smalls steps and write those small steps down and then start.....

And start you must! Breaking things down into small manageable steps will help you beat procrastination. But the thing when starting something is to simply do that – start it! Do something. Even if what you have to do is break down your first step into micro steps to fit into the time you have available then do that. But do something!

Stephen is a freelance speaker specialising in well-being, productivity, and skills for person facing work and 'knowledge' work. He is also a lecturer in Social Work at Sunderland University.

He was a practicing Social Worker for 12 years and has been a Social Work academic for 11 years. His experiences led him to explore issues relating to stress in the workplace and how to mitigate such factors through building emotional, physical, and practical resilience. He wrote about this in "How to Thrive in Professional Practice" as lead author and in "How to Thrive at Work", a reworking of the original book. The 'Professional Practice" version is aimed at Social Workers and the "Work' version at everyone.

His interest in stress and burnout in Social Work led him to conduct research for his MSc Practice Development (Social Work) into whether social work attracts a particular 'type' of person and what the implications of that are in how empathy is demonstrated.

He plays guitar, sings, and writes songs
He loves plants, dogs, and people…. In that order ;-)

Focus on... managing and getting the most from emails.